Dip in, Dad!

Written by **Liz Miles**
Illustrated by **QBS Learning**

Fast phonics

Before reading this book, ask the student to practise saying the sounds (phonemes) and reading the new words used in the book. Try to make it as speedy and as fun as possible.

Read the tricky high frequency words

The student can't sound out these words at the moment, but they need to know them because they are commonly used.

to

the   I   and

Tip: Encourage the student to sound out any sounds they know in these words, and you can provide them with the irregular or tricky part.

Say the sounds

d   g   o

n   i   p   a   t

Tip: Remember to say the pure sounds. For example, 'sssss' and 'nnnnn'. If you need a reminder, watch the *Snappy Sounds* videos.

Snappy words

Point at a word randomly and have the student read the word. The student will need to sound out the word and blend the sounds to read the word. For example: 't–o–p, top'.

on	dog	top
Dad	did	not
Dan	dip	got
tag		

Quick vocabulary check

The underlined words may not be familiar to the student. Check their understanding before you start to read the book.

Dad got on.

I did not.

Dad got to the top.

I did not.

I got to the dog and got on.

I got to the top.

Dip in, Dad!

Dad and I got in.

Comprehension questions

Let's talk about the story together
Ask the student:
- What happened at the end of the story?
- What did Dan climb on? What did Dad climb on?
- What did 'tag' mean in the game?
- Why do you think Dan didn't climb to the top with Dad?

Snappy words
Ask the student to read these words as quickly as they can.

dog	Dad	got	did
top	on	not	tag

Fluency
Can the student read the story again and improve on the last time?

Have fun!